BROTHERHOOD AWARD WINNER

We specialize in publishing quality books for
young people. For a complete list please write

LERNER PUBLICATIONS COMPANY
241 First Avenue North, Minneapolis, Minnesota 55401

Red Man, White Man, African Chief

The Story of Skin Color

By Marguerite Rush Lerner, M. D.

Illustrated by George Overlie

MEDICAL BOOKS FOR CHILDREN

LERNER PUBLICATIONS COMPANY
Minneapolis, Minnesota

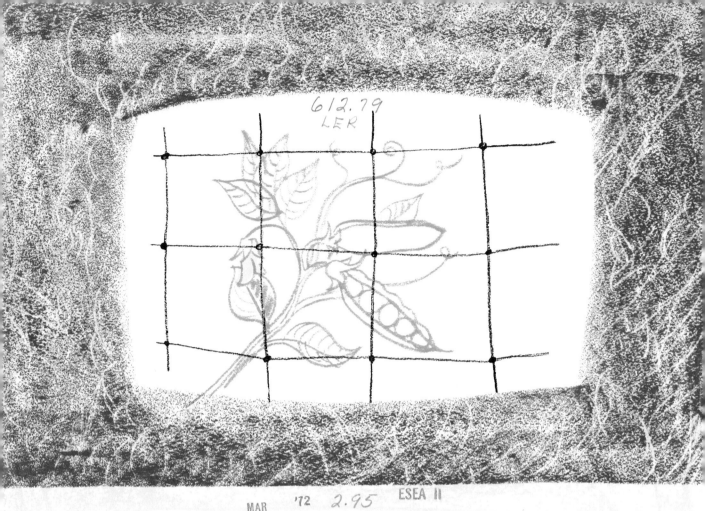

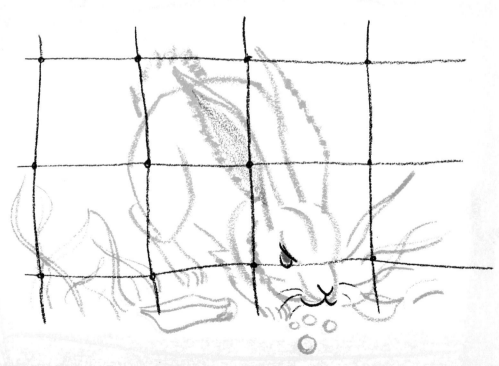

All living things have color: plants,
animals, people. The stuff that color
is made of is called pigment.
Paints are a form of pigment.

The yellow color of the buttercup
comes from the pigment,
xanthophyll *(ZAN - tha - fil)*.
Dandelions contain xanthophyll,
and so do the leaves that turn
yellow in autumn.

The orange color of the carrot comes from the

pigment, carotene *(KARE - a - teen)*.

Pumpkins contain carotene.

The green color of grass comes from the pigment,

chlorophyll *(KLOR - a - fil)*. Asparagus,

spinach and lettuce have chlorophyll.

The red color of blood comes from

the pigment, hemoglobin *(HEEM - o - globin).*

Hemoglobin contains the metal,

iron. Some rocks look red

because they contain iron, too.

What is black?

Charcoal is black. The chemical,

carbon, makes charcoal black.

Blackness of living things is

not due to carbon.

A pigment called melanin *(MEL - a - nin)*

makes living cells black or brown.

If you cut open a raw potato

and let it stand awhile, it turns

brown or black. That happens

because melanin pigment forms when

an uncooked potato is exposed to air.

A banana becomes brown
or black when it is cut open
and left out in the air or
when it is bruised. Melanin
pigment forms in the banana.
Mushrooms can make lots of melanin.

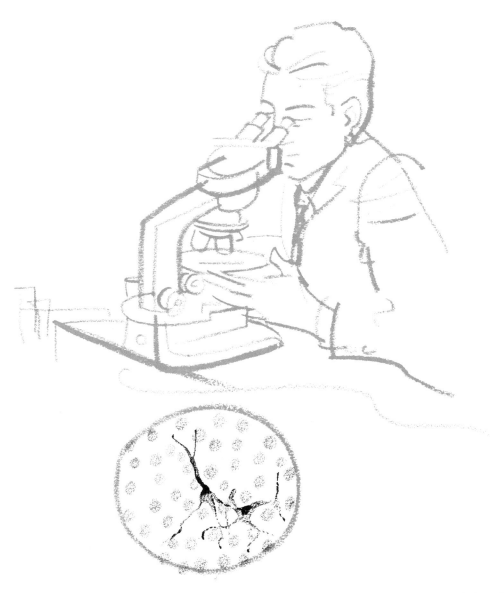

Living things are made of different kinds

of cells. Each cell has a job to do.

This is a melanocyte *(MEL - an - o - site)*.

A melanocyte is a cell that makes

melanin pigment or coloring matter.

The zebra's stripes

and the leopard's spots

are made of melanin.

The skin of the frog is spattered

with bunches of melanocytes

that look like ink blots.

People have

melanocytes, too,

in their skin,

hair roots

and eyes.

Some people have more melanin
pigment than others. Many Negroes
have a lot of melanin pigment.

Some people have very little or no
melanin pigment. They look white
and are called albinos. Other
people have in-between amounts.

The American Indian
does not have red
skin. His skin is brown
because it contains
melanin pigment.
A person is a "red man"
only if he paints his skin red.

People from China, Japan and India

do not have yellow skin.

Their skin is brown because it

contains melanin pigment.

The white man is not really

white because his skin

DOES contain melanin pigment.

When he goes out in the sun,

his skin becomes brown because

melanocytes make more pigment

during hot weather with

plenty of sunshine.

People who sit by an open fire

or who use a heating pad for a

very long time may get

brown spots on their skin.

Freckles are dark spots in the skin

that contain melanin.

They first form in children about 5 years

old after they have been out in the sun.

Freckles are darker, and there are more

of them, in the summer than in the

winter. They become less noticeable

after a person reaches the age of 25.

Moles or nevi *(NEE - vye)* are dark spots

in the skin that contain melanin. They do

not need sunlight to form. Nevi first show up

in children about 3 years old. People

get more nevi as they grow older.

All people have about the same number of melanocytes in their skin. Albinos have melanocytes, but their skin is white because they are born without a special chemical called tyrosinase *(TY - ra - si - nase)* that is needed to form melanin pigment.

Red-headed people do not suntan as well as people with blond or dark hair because they do not have enough tyrosinase needed to make pigment in their skin. Red-haired persons tend to sunburn more than to suntan. Dark skin helps protect people from strong sunlight.

Nobody knows whether the first person on earth had dark skin or light skin. We do know that in parts of the world where there is a lot of sunlight, as in Africa and India, most people have dark skin. Where there is less sun and heat, as in northern Europe and Asia and North America, most people have light skin.

Many thousands of years ago, man lived
outside more than he does now. He did
not have a house to keep out the sunshine.
It is possible that in the hot countries
people with dark skin were able to
survive because the melanin pigment in
their skin protected them against
the bright rays of the sun. In northern
countries with less sunlight people
did not need as much pigment to
stay alive. The skin color of our
ancestors who lived thousands of years ago
has been passed down to us who live today.

Usually people with light skin have children with light skin, and people with dark skin have children with dark skin. The skin that covers our bodies is like cloth. Cloth is woven from threads of many colors. The color of our skin comes from the different pigments that we get from our parents and from our ancestors of long ago.

HOW TO SAY THE WORDS

CAROTENE	*KARE - a - teen*	MELANOCYTE	*MEL - an - o - site*
CHLOROPHYLL	*KLOR - a - fil*	NEVI	*NEE - vye*
ENZYME	*EN - zyme*	TYROSINASE	*TY - ra - si - nase*
HEMOGLOBIN	*HEEM - o - globin*	TYROSINE	*TY - ra - sine*
MELANIN	*MEL - a - nin*	XANTHOPHYLL	*ZAN - tha - fil*

For Parents and Teachers

THE BIOCHEMISTRY OF SKIN COLOR

The main pigment in skin, hair and eyes is called melanin. The word melanin comes from the Greek *melas,* meaning black. Melanin is formed in pigment cells called melanocytes. Most people, even those with very light coloring, have some melanin in their skin, hair and eyes. The quantity of melanin in the skin, and its state of dispersion or scattering, determine how dark a person appears.

In the skin and eyes of albinos, in gray hair and in the skin of people with an abnormality called vitiligo, no melanin is present. In the skin of darkly pigmented or excessively suntanned people, in freckles, in nevi or moles, in black hair and in black eyes there is an abundance of melanin.

Melanin is produced from a reaction between the amino acid tyrosine and oxygen. The speed of this reaction is controlled by an enzyme or catalyst called tyrosinase that is present in the pigment cells in the skin and eyes. Tyrosine occurs in all meats and in most dairy products. Regular diets supply adequate amounts of tyrosine for melanin formation. Oxygen, obtained from the air we breathe, is carried from the lungs by hemoglobin in the blood to the pigment-producing cells. Tyrosinase, the catalyst, is a protein that is made up of many different amino acids. It is unusual in that it contains copper. The small amounts of copper we eat every day are sufficient for tyrosinase to function.

The three substances, *tyrosine, oxygen* and *tyrosinase,* combine in the melanocytes. When we expose ourselves to sunlight, a tan is produced because the ultraviolet light from the sun causes tyrosinase in the melanocytes of the skin to be more active. Consequently, more tyrosine is converted to melanin; and the skin darkens. An albino human being or animal is white because his melanocytes do not contain tyrosinase and hence cannot form melanin.

While the quantity of melanin in melanocytes is one factor that determines the color of skin, another is the state of dispersion or distribution of the melanin pigment particles in these cells. This can be shown dramatically in marine animals such as lizards, chameleons and frogs. Within a period of 1 to 60 minutes, these animals can change their skin color from dark to light and back again. This color change is *not* due to variations in the melanin content of the cell but instead to a change in the state of dispersion of the melanin particles. When particles of melanin pigment are distributed throughout the melanocytes, the skin looks dark. When melanin particles are clumped tightly in the center of the cell, the skin looks light. This concept can be made clear by the following analogy.

If a small piece of coal is placed at the center of a large, white table, the table top will appear white except at the center where the coal is. If the coal is then ground to a very fine powder, and this black powder is sprinkled uniformly over the entire surface of the table, the table top will look black. Although the amount of coal on the table did not change, the table top changed in color from white to black because there was a change in the distribution or dispersion of the coal particles on the surface of the table.

In man this dispersion effect usually is not as important or dramatic as it is in some marine animals such as frogs. Nevertheless, it seems significant. The darkening of the face of women in the latter part of pregnancy probably is due to this dispersion effect. Hormones from the pituitary gland in the brain also can darken skin in this manner.

The color of skin, hair and eyes is determined by the net balance of the factors that control the formation of melanin and its dispersion in melanocytes. These factors in turn are dependent upon genetic and environmental regulation.

The author is shown receiving the Brotherhood Award from school teacher - comedian Sam Levenson

MARGUERITE RUSH LERNER, M.D., lives with her husband and four sons in Connecticut. Dr. Lerner's first academic degree was earned in English literature at the University of Minnesota. She attended Barnard College for pre-medical work, studied medicine at Johns Hopkins and Western Reserve universities and completed her clinical training at the University of Michigan and University of Oregon hospitals. She is an assistant clinical professor of dermatology at Yale University School of Medicine.

She became interested in explaining the story of skin color to children while hearing and learning about the work of her husband, Dr. Aaron Lerner. He is professor of dermatology at Yale and has done biochemical research and clinical studies on pigmentation in human beings and is a recognized authority in this field.